Francis Frith's
CHESHIRE

PHOTOGRAPHIC MEMORIES

Francis Frith's
CHESHIRE

◆

Clive Hardy

FRITH
BOOK Co

First published in the United Kingdom in 1999 by
Frith Book Company Ltd

Hardback Edition 1999
ISBN 1-85937-045-4

Paperback Edition 2001
ISBN 1-85937-271-6

Hardback Reprinted in 2001

British Library Cataloguing in Publication Data

Francis Frith's Cheshire
Clive Hardy

Frith Book Company Ltd
Frith's Barn, Teffont,
Salisbury, Wiltshire SP3 5QP
Tel: +44 (0) 1722 716 376
Email: info@frithbook.co.uk
www.frithbook.co.uk

Printed and bound in Great Britain

AS WITH ANY HISTORICAL DATABASE THE FRITH ARCHIVE IS CONSTANTLY BEING CORRECTED AND IMPROVED
AND THE PUBLISHERS WOULD WELCOME INFORMATION ON OMISSIONS OR INACCURACIES

CONTENTS

FRANCIS FRITH: *Victorian Pioneer*

FRANCIS FRITH, Victorian founder of the world-famous photographic archive, was a complex and multitudinous man. A devout Quaker and a highly successful Victorian businessman, he was both philosophic by nature and pioneering in outlook.

By 1855 Francis Frith had already established a wholesale grocery business in Liverpool, and sold it for the astonishing sum of £200,000, which is the equivalent today of over £15,000,000. Now a multi-millionaire, he was able to indulge his passion for travel. As a child he had pored over travel books written by early explorers, and his fancy and imagination had been stirred by family holidays to the sublime mountain regions of Wales and Scotland. 'What a land of spirit-stirring and enriching scenes and places!' he had written. He was to return to these scenes of grandeur in later years to 'recapture the thousands of vivid and tender memories', but with a different purpose. Now in his thirties, and captivated by the new science of photography, Frith set out on a series of pioneering journeys to the Nile regions that occupied him from 1856 until 1860.

INTRIGUE AND ADVENTURE

He took with him on his travels a specially-designed wicker carriage that acted as both dark-room and sleeping chamber. These far-flung journeys were packed with intrigue and adventure. In his life story, written when he was sixty-three, Frith tells of being held captive by bandits, and of fighting 'an awful midnight battle to the very point of surrender with a deadly pack of hungry, wild dogs'. Sporting flowing Arab costume, Frith arrived at Akaba by camel seventy years before Lawrence, where he encountered 'desert princes and rival sheikhs, blazing with jewel-hilted swords'.

During these extraordinary adventures he was assiduously exploring the desert regions bordering the Nile and patiently recording the antiquities and peoples with his camera. He was the first photographer to venture beyond the sixth cataract. Africa was still the mysterious 'Dark Continent', and Stanley and Livingstone's historic meeting was a decade into the future. The conditions for picture taking confound belief. He laboured for hours in his wicker dark-room in the sweltering heat of the desert, while the volatile chemicals fizzed dangerously in their trays. Often he was forced to work in remote tombs and caves where conditions were cooler. Back in London he exhibited his photographs and was 'rapturously cheered' by members of the Royal Society. His reputation as a photographer was made overnight. An eminent modern historian has likened their impact on the population of the time to that on our own generation of the first photographs taken on the surface of the moon.

VENTURE OF A LIFE-TIME

Characteristically, Frith quickly spotted the opportunity to create a new business as a specialist publisher of photographs. He lived in an era of immense and sometimes violent change. For the poor in the early part of Victoria's reign work was a drudge and the hours long, and people had precious little free time to enjoy themselves.

Most had no transport other than a cart or gig at their disposal, and had not travelled far beyond the boundaries of their own town or village. However, by the 1870s, the railways had threaded their way across the country, and Bank Holidays and half-day Saturdays had been made obligatory by Act of Parliament. All of a sudden the ordinary working man and his family were able to enjoy days out and see a little more of the world.

With characteristic business acumen, Francis Frith foresaw that these new tourists would enjoy having souvenirs to commemorate their days out. In 1860 he married Mary Ann Rosling and set out with the intention of photographing every city, town and village in Britain. For the next thirty years he travelled the country by train and by pony and trap, producing fine photographs of seaside resorts and beauty spots that were keenly bought by millions of Victorians. These prints were painstakingly pasted into family albums and pored over during the dark nights of winter, rekindling precious memories of summer excursions.

THE RISE OF FRITH & CO

Frith's studio was soon supplying retail shops all over the country. To meet the demand he gathered about him a small team of photographers, and published the work of independent artist-photographers of the calibre of Roger Fenton and Francis Bedford. In order to gain some understanding of the scale of Frith's business one only has to look at the catalogue issued by Frith & Co in 1886: it runs to some 670

court card, but there was little room for illustration. In 1899, a year after Frith's death, a new card measuring 5.5 x 3.5 inches became the standard format, but it was not until 1902 that the divided back came into being, with address and message on one face and a full-size illustration on the other. *Frith & Co* were in the vanguard of postcard development, and Frith's sons Eustace and Cyril continued their father's monumental task, expanding the number of views offered to the public and recording more and more places in Britain, as the coasts and countryside were opened up to mass travel.

Francis Frith died in 1898 at his villa in Cannes, his great project still growing. The archive he created continued in business for another seventy years. By 1970 it contained over a third of a million pictures of 7,000 cities, towns and villages. The massive photographic record Frith has left to us stands as a living monument to a special and very remarkable man.

pages, listing not only many thousands of views of the British Isles but also many photographs of most European countries, and China, Japan, the USA and Canada – note the sample page shown above from the hand-written *Frith & Co* ledgers detailing pictures taken. By 1890 Frith had created the greatest specialist photographic publishing company in the world, with over 2,000 outlets – more than the combined number that Boots and WH Smith have today! The picture on the right shows the *Frith & Co* display board at Ingleton in the Yorkshire Dales. Beautifully constructed with mahogany frame and gilt inserts, it could display up to a dozen local scenes.

POSTCARD BONANZA

◆

The ever-popular holiday postcard we know today took many years to develop. In 1870 the Post Office issued the first plain cards, with a pre-printed stamp on one face. In 1894 they allowed other publishers' cards to be sent through the mail with an attached adhesive halfpenny stamp. Demand grew rapidly, and in 1895 a new size of postcard was permitted called the

Frith's Archive: *A Unique Legacy*

FRANCIS FRITH'S legacy to us today is of immense significance and value, for the magnificent archive of evocative photographs he created provides a unique record of change in 7,000 cities, towns and villages throughout Britain over a century and more. Frith and his fellow studio photographers revisited locations many times down the years to update their views, compiling for us an enthralling and colourful pageant of British life and character.

We tend to think of Frith's sepia views of Britain as nostalgic, for most of us use them to conjure up memories of places in our own lives with which we have family associations. It often makes us forget that to Francis Frith they were records of daily life as it was actually being lived in the cities, towns and villages of his day. The Victorian age was one of great and often bewildering change for ordinary people, and though the pictures evoke an impression of slower times, life was as busy and hectic as it is today.

We are fortunate that Frith was a photographer of the people, dedicated to recording the minutiae of everyday life. For it is this sheer wealth of visual data, the painstaking chronicle of changes in dress, transport, street layouts, buildings, housing, engineering and landscape that captivates us so much today. His remarkable images offer us a powerful link with the past and with the lives of our ancestors.

TODAY'S TECHNOLOGY

Computers have now made it possible for Frith's many thousands of images to be accessed almost instantly. In the Frith archive today, each photograph is carefully 'digitised' then stored on a CD Rom. Frith archivists can locate a single photograph amongst thousands within seconds. Views can be catalogued and sorted under a variety of categories of place and content to the immediate benefit of researchers. Inexpensive reference prints can be created for them at the touch of a mouse button, and a wide range of books and other printed materials assembled and published for a wider, more general readership - in the next twelve months over a hundred Frith local history titles will be published! The

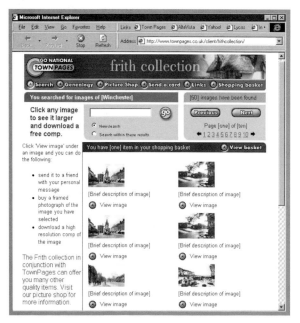

See Frith at www. francisfrith.co.uk

day-to-day workings of the archive are very different from how they were in Francis Frith's time: imagine the herculean task of sorting through eleven tons of glass negatives as Frith had to do to locate a particular sequence of pictures! Yet the archive still prides itself on maintaining the same high standards of excellence laid down by Francis Frith, including the painstaking cataloguing and indexing of every view.

It is curious to reflect on how the internet now allows researchers in America and elsewhere greater instant access to the archive than Frith himself ever enjoyed. Many thousands of individual views can be called up on screen within seconds on one of the Frith internet sites, enabling people living continents away to revisit the streets of their ancestral home town, or view places in Britain where they have enjoyed holidays. Many overseas researchers welcome the chance to view special theme selections, such as transport, sports, costume and ancient monuments.

We are certain that Francis Frith would have heartily approved of these modern developments, for he himself was always working at the very limits of Victorian photographic technology.

THE VALUE OF THE ARCHIVE TODAY

Because of the benefits brought by the computer, Frith's images are increasingly studied by social historians, by researchers into genealogy and ancestory, by architects, town planners, and by teachers and schoolchildren involved in local history projects. In addition, the archive offers every one of us a unique opportunity to examine the places where we and our families have lived and worked down the years. Immensely successful in Frith's own era, the archive is now, a century and more on, entering a new phase of popularity.

THE PAST IN TUNE WITH THE FUTURE

Historians consider the Francis Frith Collection to be of prime national importance. It is the only archive of its kind remaining in private ownership and has been valued at a million pounds. However, this figure is now rapidly increasing as digital technology enables more and more people around the world to enjoy its benefits.

Francis Frith's archive is now housed in an historic timber barn in the beautiful village of Teffont in Wiltshire. Its founder would not recognize the archive office as it is today. In place of the many thousands of dusty boxes containing glass plate negatives and an all-pervading odour of photographic chemicals, there are now ranks of computer screens. He would be amazed to watch his images travelling round the world at unimaginable speeds through network and internet lines.

The archive's future is both bright and exciting. Francis Frith, with his unshakeable belief in making photographs available to the greatest number of people, would undoubtedly approve of what is being done today with his lifetime's work. His photographs, depicting our shared past, are now bringing pleasure and enlightenment to millions around the world a century and more after his death.

CHESHIRE – *An Introduction*

THE NAME Cheshire first appears in written records in AD980 as 'Legeceasterscir', the 'shire of the city of the legions'. It is thought to date back to around the year AD920, when it is believed that the county was created by Edward the Elder of Wessex in the months following his seizing of the Mercian throne from his niece Aelfwyn. For part of the tenth century Cheshire was a frontier zone. To the north, across the Mersey, lay the territory of Northumbria, under Danish rule and controlled from York. To the east, across the Derbyshire Pennines, was the western border of the Danelaw, created by a treaty between Alfred the Great and Guthrum; this embraced East Anglia, Essex and a part of Mercia. To the west, there lay the independent Welsh kingdom of Gwynedd.

CHESTER

It was during the campaigns against the Brigantes and the Welsh that the strategic importance of the site now occupied by Chester was seen clearly by the Romans. The campaigns had led to the full-scale occupation of Cheshire; the Roman army needed a secure base of operations from which they could control the north-west of the country, whilst at the same time maintaining their own lines of communication. The site was on the north bank of the Dee at the lowest bridging point before the estuary. Covering 56 acres, the fortress comprised an outer ditch, a turfed rampart topped by a wooden palisade, together with wooden gatehouses and towers. Capable of holding a legion, the huge fortress was completed in AD79-80, but at some time around AD100 reconstruction work began to make Deva, as it was called, a more permanent establishment. The XX Legion was here to stay.

A new ditch system was dug, and locally quarried stone replaced wooden defences. The fortress contained the usual buildings associated with an important military installation: headquarters, barracks, bath house, latrines, hospital, gymnasium, granaries, workshops, storage and equipment sheds. A civilian settlement grew up outside the walls and stretched along what is now Foregate Street. Also outside the walls, to the south-east, was the amphitheatre, which was capable of holding 8000 spectators.

During the Roman period, the estuary of the Dee extended almost to the city of Chester. On the edge of what is now the Roodee they built wharfs and warehouses and there might even have been a naval jetty, though anchorage for the main fleet's operations in the Irish Sea would probably have been located further along the estuary.

Little is known about life in Chester following the final withdrawal of troops and the collapse of Roman authority. We do know that in some towns local authorities remained identifiably Roman for many years; others

Cheshire remained under Northumbrian control until AD633, when defeat at the hands of the combined forces of Mercia and Gwynedd pushed them back over the Mersey. Inspired by the victory, Mercia embarked upon its own quest for territorial expansion, followed by consolidation. To the western border, defences known as Wat's Dyke, were built by King Penda in the seventh century, followed by Offa's Dyke in the latter quarter of the eighth century. However, Chester does not appear to have been refortified until around AD907, when the northern and east-

were little better than ghost towns with only a fraction of their former area remaining occupied. According to Bede, Chester enjoyed the status of a civitas, implying that it was still an important centre, and we do know that a synod was held there around AD607. It was considered important enough by Aethelfrith of Northumbria for him to launch an all-out assault and destroy the place during his conquest of the area in about AD616. The Northumbrians are also believed to have massacred 1200 monks at the nearby Celtic monastery of Bangor-is-y-Coed.

ern walls were rehabilitated as part of a defensive strategy against the renewed threat from Northumbria. Over the next fifteen years or so, the northern border was strengthened by the establishment of fortified burghs at Eddisbury, Runcorn, Thelwell and Manchester.

Edward the Elder's seizing of the Mercian throne might be considered the tidying up of a few loose ends. By AD920, the power of the Danelaw had been smashed by Edward of Wessex, and he was grudgingly acknowledged as overlord by the Northumbrians. However, the idea of a unified England did not sit well with the people of Cheshire, who rose in armed revolt in AD922 and joined forces with the Welsh. Edward died at Farndon in AD924, still attempting to bring Cheshire to heel. The new king was Athelstan. Daring, resourceful, and, when necessary, totally ruthless, this soldier-politician invaded Northumbria and Scotland, and in AD937 destroyed a combined Scots, Danish and Welsh army at Brunanburgh, which might be modern Bromborough. Following Athelstan's victory there was a short period of peace, but the king died in AD939 and old antagonisms re-emerged. Northumbria again asserted itself, and was not finally being brought back into anything like a unified country until AD955.

Chester at this time was the most important city in the northwest. It was a centre for trade and commerce, and there was a mint. In AD972 Chester was chosen by King Edgar as the most suitable place to engage in a set piece of power politics when he was rowed along the Dee by eight Celtic kings and chief-

tains. The concept of a unified England was still new, and the reigns of the last of the Viking kings of York and Northumbrian attempts at re-establishing independence were well within living memory. This act of submission by these kings was Edgar's way of letting all know just who was High King. Unfortunately, Edgar died in AD975 and once again the country was plunged into a period of instability.

For a time, Chester was used by Ethelred the Unready as a base for operations against Norse raiders. Throughout Ethelred's reign England was plagued by Danish raids; in AD994 he attempted to buy them off with money raised by the Danegeld. It worked for a while, but in AD997 they were back. Raising massive amounts of money every year to pay off the Danes proved to be too much, and was a direct cause of the massacre of thousands of peaceful Danish settlers in 1002. Retaliation came in 1013 when England fell to King Sweyn. Sweyn's rule lasted only a few months, and on his death Ethelred was restored to the throne. On Ethelred's death in 1016 Sweyn's

son Cnut became king.

It was during Ethelred's reign that Chester became the capital of what in effect was a semi-independent land, free from royal control and ruled by the earls of Mercia. As well as Cheshire, the earls held sway over Staffordshire and Shropshire, and apart from an attempt by Edmund Ironside to restore the royal writ, the three counties enjoyed their autonomous status until the eve of the Norman Conquest. The Norman Conquest did not end with the Battle of Hastings. There were a number of uprisings, including one in Cheshire, in 1069. They were ruthlessly put down; whole villages were destroyed and the people massacred. In 1070 Chester was occupied and much of the city was destroyed.

In 1071 William the Conqueror conferred a new title, that of Earl of Chester, on his nephew, Hugh of Avranches, and he and his successors would be major figures not only within Cheshire, but also in the government of England, for the next 160 years. The Normans secured their hold on Cheshire by building a number of castles at strategic points around the county as well as a line of castles along the western border with Wales.

During the 12th and 13th centuries the population of the county grew rapidly, resulting in more land being turned over to agriculture. Because of the damp climate it is likely that the majority of crops were oats and barley, both of which would have little difficulty in thriving in the fertile soil of the plain. To this day farming is still an important industry in the county.

THE OLD INDUSTRIES

Industry came early to Cheshire. We now know that copper ore was being extracted from Alderley Edge as early as 2,000BC. The Edge itself is a wooded sandstone cliff stretching some two miles in length and rising to around 650ft. The discovery of a number of flint implements and a readily available water supply suggest that the Edge has been occupied since ancient times. There are also a number of surface workings, such as those at Stormy Point, which are thought to date from the Bronze Age when copper ore was extracted from the sandstone. During the Roman occupation it is thought that copper ore was transported from the Edge to workshops at Wilderspool near present day Warrington. It is unclear if the copper deposits were being worked during the Middle Ages, as there is as yet no reliable evidence for mining operations prior to 1693. Copper was mined during the 18th century, though the most intense period appears to have been between 1857 and 1877 when about 250,000 tons of ore was extracted. However, the industry went into decline, unable to compete with foreign imports.

The salt springs around present-day Northwich and Middlewich have been worked since at least the fifth century BC, but it was the Romans who developed the industry by exploiting these deposits and those at Nantwich, Shavington, Tetton and Moston. Of these, Northwich, Middlewich and Nantwich would prove to be the most important, not just to the Romans, but to their successors in the centuries following the collapse of the Western Empire.

Northwich (Condate) and Middlewich (Salinae) were both garrisoned by the Romans during the late first century. The forts at both towns were situated close to major road junctions, but it is also possible that these installations served in the additional role of protecting any business interests that the Roman Army might have in the area. It was standard practice throughout the empire for army units to develop business interests in the areas they garrisoned; lead-mining, quarrying, slaves, vineyards, farming, trapping wild animals to appear in the circus - whatever was appropriate. It would not have been unreasonable for the XX Legion to have taken an interest in the salt workings and to have used these two forts to help regulate trade and collect dues. Salt working survived the collapse of Roman rule, and by the

brine-springs, the water being pumped into large shallow iron pans and then boiled to leave salt crystals. However, the continuous pumping of brine has resulted in many buildings in and around Northwich suffering from subsidence and structural damage. The natural brown rock-salt of the area is not as pure as the table salt and is now mainly used for spreading on the roads in winter.

The first rock-salt to be discovered in England was on the Marbury Estate at Marston, Northwich in 1670. The find was purely accidental, as the prospectors, led by one John Jackson, were in fact looking for coal. Commercial mining of the deposit

late Saxon period Northwich, Middlewich and Nantwich benefited from their high status. When the Domesday Book was being compiled the salt industry of Cheshire was considered important enough for a detailed account to be entered, including fines to be levied for the overloading of carts and packhorses. For centuries Northwich's prosperity was based on the mining of salt. The town's motto is Sal est Vita, Salt is Life.

White household salt is produced from

began in 1682 and lasted for nearly forty years until the workings were flooded. By the 1780s miners were going ever deeper in search of purer salt, and by 1808 workings extended over many acres and to a great depth.

At the beginning of the Second World War there were several salt mines in operation at Winsford. The biggest was that belonging to the Salt Union, whose facility stretched along the banks of the Weaver from Winsford to Meadow Bank where the large evaporation pans for producing table salt were situated. The Salt Union eventually became a part of ICI, and though salt is still mined, the banks of the Weaver are lined with the remains of buildings and derelict loading staithes.

Thanks to the Weaver Navigation, Northwich also developed as a centre for the building and repairing of narrow boats, barges and small seagoing ships such as tugs. The industry flourished for over two hundred years, and though the British Waterways Board Yard is still very active, the last private shipyard, Pimblott's, closed in 1971 because of foreign competition.

During the Civil War, Sir William Brereton, commander-in-chief of Parliamentary forces in Cheshire, Shropshire and Staffordshire, established his headquarters at Nantwich; the town was used as the base of operations for an assault on Chester in July 1643. On Boxing Day 1643, Lord Byron left Chester with a force comprising 2000 horse and 300 foot, intending to lay siege to Nantwich and bottle-up Brereton behind his defences. However, Brereton moved out of Nantwich and clashed with Byron's troops along the road to Middlewich. It was a brisk engagement in which Brereton was driven from the field; the survivors of his command fell back on Nantwich. In another incident that day, the Parliamentary garrison holding Barthomley Church were massacred.

The weather now played its part in the proceedings. Heavy snowfalls in some parts of the country hampered military operations, and it was not until 21 January 1644 that Sir Thomas Fairfax arrived in Manchester en route to relieve Nantwich. Three days later, Fairfax made his move. He was intercepted by a Royalist detachment in Delamare Forest but quickly brushed them aside. It was then that nature played its hand. Thawing snow caused the Weaver to burst its banks, effectively splitting the Royalist forces in two. Fairfax struck,

inflicting heavy casualties and routing Byron.

In 1698 when the traveller Celia Fiennes visited Nantwich, a brine-shaft said to date from before the Roman occupation was still being worked. Old Biot, as it was called, continued in production until just after the end of the Napoleonic Wars, and in 1883 the site was used for a medicinal baths. The baths included private hot brine baths and a swimming pool, and the therapeutic qualities of the water were similar to those at Droitwich Spa. For those who wished to bath in the privacy of their own homes, Nantwich brine was dispatched in casks. The manufacture of salt ceased in 1847; over 250 shafts and mines have been located in and around the town.

EAST TO NORTH

Situated between Congleton and Macclesfield, Gawsworth, the seat of the Fytton family for over four centuries, is famous for its timber-framed Old Hall. In a wood near the church is the tomb of Maggoty Johnson, a dancing-master turned eccentric fiddle-player and playwright. One of his operas ran in London for a month or more, encouraging Maggoty to write another three plays. Failing to secure backing, he returned to Gawsworth, where he died in 1773 aged 82, having ordered that he be buried as far away as possible from the vulgar gentry of London who had failed to appreciate his genius.

By the eleventh century, the village of Macclesfield boasted a water mill, had over a thousand acres of land under cultivation, and along with the village of Adlington was the most valuable piece of land in east Cheshire. Both settlements were owned by Earl Edwin of Mercia. In 1069, disaster struck when

Macclesfield was destroyed by the Normans, during their offensive to put down an uprising in northern England. Even twenty years after this calamitous event, the total manpower of the settlement was recorded as being just four serfs. But Macclesfield did recover. It became the administrative centre for the Hundred, Manor and Forest of Macclesfield: the Forest Court was held in the village.

The medieval forest was not necessarily a wooded area: it was a district mainly reserved for hunting, but could and did include isolated farms, hamlets (such as Pott Shrigley), and limited grazing for sheep and cattle. Around the year 1220 Ranulf, Earl of Chester and Lord of the Manor of Macclesfield, granted a charter commuting the servile dues of 120 villeins in return for an annual payment. In 1261 Prince Edward, eldest son of Henry III, granted the place the status of a free borough, with the right to have its own merchant guild, and exempted the burgesses from various taxes, tolls and duties, except those on salt.

During the 16th century the town became a centre for button-making, though the earliest reference to the manufacture of silk buttons dates from 1649. This cottage industry spread to surrounding villages, and trade connections enabled local merchants to

diversify into supplying silk thread for the London market and later into other silk goods. By the last quarter of the 18th century, the town enjoyed a lucrative export trade to the American colonies, Holland and even to Russia. In 1765 it was estimated that in and around Macclesfield some 12,000 to 15,000 people were employed in the silk industry as a whole. Some were working in the new factories, while others still worked from home. In 1743 Charles Roe erected a mill for silk throwing using water-powered machinery, originally of Italian design, but brought to England in 1715 by John Lombe of Derby. Roe's mill was a success and others soon opened.

But the Macclesfield silk industry would always be a tale of boom and bust. The years immediately following the end of the Seven Years War saw a major slump. Roe might well have seen the writing on the wall. He sold out his interests for around £10,000 in 1763, and went off to do other things. His original partners went bust in 1773. The Napoleonic Wars led to a revival in fortunes, and trade expanded at the expense of the French silk industry. Silk weaving had been introduced around 1790, and by 1817 the town had twelve manufacturers of woven silk. The end

the fledgling canal network. In 1766 a Bill was presented for a canal from Witton Bridge to Macclesfield, Stockport and from there to Manchester. Needless to say, the Duke of Bridgewater scuppered the Bill in the Lords to protect his own interests. Charles Roe died in 1781, but the Macclesfield smelter contin-

of the war saw the industry depressed once more, but it picked up again during the 1820s.

At one time Macclesfield also boasted a copper smelting works. It was established around 1758 by Charles Roe and his brother-in-law Rowland Atkinson, who was the headmaster of the local grammar school. Local supplies of raw materials were limited: there was a coal deposit on the common and copper ore at Alderley Edge. Neither amounted to much, and Roe imported copper ore from Coniston and coal from Norbury and Wrexham. But the venture was a success, and Roe became a very wealthy man. He expanded the business, opening smelters at Havanna, Bosley and Liverpool.

Roe was also one of the leading lights behind a scheme to get Macclesfield linked to

ued in production until 1801, when it was offered for sale. There were no takers, and the works was eventually demolished.

Though the silk industry had been established in Macclesfield, Bollington and Congleton, the late 18th century saw the opening of cotton mills in northeast Cheshire, the first being at Staleybridge in 1776. Macclesfield got its first cotton mill in 1785, and by the end of the French Wars there were six within the borough, plus two in Old Mill Lane, and one at Hurdsfield. The mills were early users of steam power. Dainty & Ryle equipped their cotton mill at Park Green with a Boulton & Watt steam engine in 1801. But, as with the silk industry, the price of peace was a manufacturing slump, and in Macclesfield the cotton industry all but collapsed. Former cotton workers had little choice but to seek employment at any price, and this pressure forced wages down in the silk industry.

THE WIRRAL

◆

Wallasey's name is derived from 'Wallas-eig', or 'the island of the Welshman', rather apt considering that there was water on three sides whilst on the fourth was marshland prone to flooding. Though fishing was the principal industry in the village, James Stonehouse, who knew the area in the late 17th century, portrayed the inhabitants as a shifty lot who made their real livings by wrecking and smuggling. He wrote that 'the inhabitants were nearly all wreckers and smugglers - they ostensibly carried on the trade and calling of fishermen, farm-labourers, and small farmers; but they were deeply saturated with the sins of covetousness, and many a fierce fire has been lighted on the Wirral shore on stormy nights to lure the good ships on the Burbo or Hoyle Banks. There is scarcely a

house in the north Wirral that could not provide a guest with a good stiff glass of brandy or Hollands'. Perhaps that explains why once, when St Hilary's burnt down, it was said that the flames had the blue haze of burning brandy.

A small Benedictine priory was founded at Birkenhead by Hamon de Massey. The Black Monks enjoyed certain fishing rights, anchorage fees and the rights of wreck and wreckage. In 1275 Edward Longshanks stayed at the priory whilst campaigning against the Welsh, and again in 1277 while he awaited the arrival of envoys of Alexander III of Scotland.

Edward II granted the priory the rights to build a lodging house for travellers using the ferry, but it was in 1330 that the monks got their hands on the ferry service itself, thanks to a charter granted by Edward III. The right of ferryage from Birkenhead to Liverpool was granted in perpetuity, and the gilded crowns on the top of the ferry gangways declare that it still operates under royal mandate. Being a

small priory, Birkenhead was one of the first to go at the Dissolution; the prior himself was pensioned off at £12 a year.

Around the end of the Napoleonic Wars, Birkenhead had a population of just over 100; by 1821 the population had doubled as the village enjoyed a brief career as a health resort. Modern Birkenhead owes its origins to William Laird, who chose a site on the north shore of Wallasey Pool as the place to build his iron and boiler works. With a steam ferry operating across the Mersey and the possibilities of employment at Lairds, Birkenhead grew so that by 1851 the population had rocketed to nearly 25,000.

In 1827 Thomas Telford and George Stephenson were part of a consortium that proposed to dredge Wallasey Pool, build a wall across its mouth and construct a ship canal across the Wirral to the Dee near Hoylake. The attraction of the scheme was that the canal and docks would be able to undercut the heavy harbour dues charged by Liverpool Corporation. In one of those classic spoiling actions with which 19th-century business enterprise is littered, Liverpool Corporation quietly spent £150,000 buying up land along the line of march, thereby scuppering the project. But by 1843 Liverpool Corporation had no further use for its Wirral territory and offered it for sale with rights to build docks. While the Corporation had in mind nothing bigger than a couple of graving docks, William Laird's son and William Jackson had other ideas. They bought the land, and construction of the Egerton and Morpeth Docks began. The docks opened in 1847, the first cargo being a ship load of guano from Patagonia. The Wirral might not have its ship canal, but

Liverpool now had a rival just three quarters of a mile away across the river.

In 1860 George Francis Train, born in Boston, America, in 1829, was already a very wealthy man, having made his money operating fast clipper ships. In that year, he came to Liverpool to negotiate with the Corporation to allow him his other passion in life: street tramways. By a strange coincidence, a tramway of sorts was already operating in Liverpool. A man by the name of William Curtis was running a horse-drawn passenger vehicle along the rails of the Mersey Docks & Harbour Board. Liverpool wasn't interested, so George took the ferry and went to see the powers that be in Birkenhead. The response was totally different. For a start, John Laird was hooked straight away, and no doubt the chance to get one over on Liverpool was not lost on the Birkenhead authorities. On 7 May 1860 the Birkenhead Street Railway Co. was registered, and just a few weeks later, on 30 August, the system was officially opened. The line was only 1.25 miles long, but it ran from the Woodside Ferry, along Argyle Street and Conway Street to Birkenhead Park. On the first day it carried 4,360 passengers. No doubt eager to expand onto the continent, Train had taken the liberty of inviting all the crowned heads of Europe, the Pope, and Garibaldi to the official opening and banquet. Alas, none of them turned up, but at least George did get a reply from Queen Victoria.

William and Agnes Laird had five sons. The second son, Macgregor, took part in the expedition led by Richard Lander to explore the Niger and examine its potential for providing access for shipping into the interior of West Africa. Out of the party of 48 men, including two doctors, 39 died, but they did prove that it was navigable to sea-going ships as far at Rabbah, some 500 miles inland.

One last Laird clan venture worth a mention here concerns the iron paddle steamer Nemesis. Though some iron ships could be built more cheaply than wooden ones, and though their watertight compartments and double hulls made them an attractive proposition from the point of view of insurance, they were proving hard to market in the late 1830s. Admiralty contracts were slow in materializing, so Laird built the Nemesis in secret. Though she was registered as a merchantman under Laird's ownership, she was sent out to China where she operated almost as a privateer during the war of 1840-42. The book written about her exploits in the war extolled the advantages of iron ships and led to increased orders for such vessels.

Without doubt, William Lever's Port Sunlight ranks alongside Titus Salt's Saltaire as an example of a benevolent employer providing a standard of housing for his workers far better than they would otherwise have been able to acquire. Port Sunlight was never

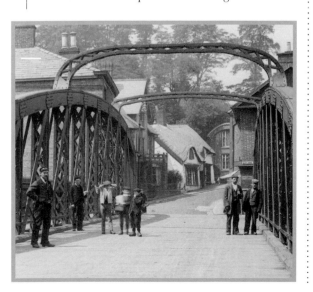

Lever's first choice. He was a Lancastrian, and only came to the Wirral after failing to find a suitable location around Warrington. Lever always knew what he wanted: 'Houses in which our workpeople will be able to live and be comfortable, houses with gardens back and front, and in which they will be able to know more about the science of life than they can in any back slum'. Lever, like Titus Salt, was also a realist. They both knew that well-housed workers offered better productivity and were better motivated, and that the number of hours lost through absenteeism would thus fall. Everyone benefited. Lever purchased 56 acres of land at £200 per acre, 24 for the factory, the remainder for the village. The first sod was cut on 1 March 1888, and with a housing density of only seven per acre more land was soon required. The village would eventually cover 130 acres and have a population in excess of 4,000. Port Sunlight was provided with its own cottage hospital, post office, library, schools and shops. There was a large general store operated along co-op lines by the Workers' Provident Society, a technical institute offering evening classes and leisure facilities, and it included an open-air swimming pool and gymnasium.

ARRIVALS AND DEPARTURES

The majority of the photographs in this book were taken between 1890 and the outbreak of the Great War. Since then, Cheshire has undergone many changes, including those to its boundaries. In 1931 Manchester was allowed to annex Northenden, Northen Etchells and Baguley, and five years later Taxal was transferred to Derbyshire, though Ludworth and Mellor were handed over in exchange. The biggest shake-up came in 1974. The metropolitan areas of Manchester and Merseyside effectively robbed Cheshire of much of its territory in the northeast and northwest of the county. Gone was the whole of the Wirral, together with the likes of Staleybridge, Sale, Altrincham and Langdendale, the latter having been given to Derbyshire. Into the county came Warrington and Widnes. Lancashire Life ran a competition to see which reader could come up with the most appropriate word to describe what was happening to their county. The winner was 'Lancastration'.

Warrington is an industrial town on the north bank of the Mersey, and was for centuries the gateway into Lancashire. Much to the annoyance of many of its inhabitants, Warrington was ceded to Cheshire during the local government's reorganization of 1974. In October 1642 the town was garrisoned by Royalist troops along with Preston, Ormskirk, Wigan, Eccleston and Prescot. On 5 April 1643 Sir William Brereton attacked the town, but his troops were unable to break through the defences and were eventually forced to withdraw. Two months later, on 20 June, the town was again the target of a Parliamentary attack, but this time it developed into a full-scale siege. Using troops from the Manchester garrison and a large part of Brereton's command, the town was effectively surrounded. The siege lasted until the 27th, when the Royalist commander Colonel Norris was granted surrender terms. Warrington then remained in Parliament's hands until the end of the war. The war ended on 5 May 1646 when the king surren-

dered to the Scottish army at Southwell, leaving only Oxford, Pendennis Castle, Raglan Castle and Harlech Castle flying the Royal Standard. Over the next few months these too surrendered, and that should have been an end to the matter. However, in 1648 fighting broke out once more: the Duke of Hamilton crossed into England with 3,000 horse and 6,000 foot. Between 17 and 19 August, Cromwell clashed with Hamilton at Preston. Though the Royalists fought well, they were pushed back. The decision was taken to fall back on Warrington, where the Scots intended to regroup and make a stand. However, they were caught by Cromwell at Winwick and prevented from doing so. Following the battle, Cromwell came to Warrington and lodged in the town.

The town was also the home of the Warrington Academy, founded in 1757 as an institute of higher education for the sons of Dissenters. One pupil, Thomas Threkeld, who later became a dissenting minister himself, appears to have had a remarkable memory. He not only knew the Bible inside out and back to front, but he could tell you where any quote was to be found: 'those verses are in the 83rd Psalm and 7th verse'.

By 1796, trade was such that 42 boats were operating between Liverpool and Manchester, including two passage boats that connected with stagecoach services. The boats left Manchester at eight in the morning and connected with the Liverpool stagecoach at Warrington. From there they navigated to Frodsham, where they met with the Chester stage.

CONGLETON, TOWN HALL 1898 42155
Here are kept the seals of office used by John Bradshaw, who became Lord President of the High Court and took part in the trial of Charles I. It was Bradshaw and his tribunal that sentenced the King to death as a tyrant and traitor.

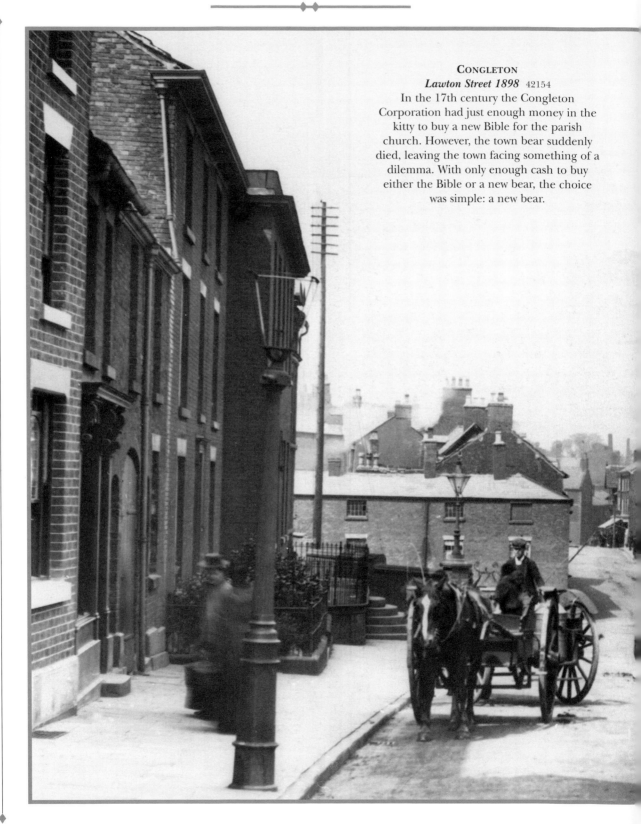

CONGLETON
Lawton Street 1898 42154
In the 17th century the Congleton
Corporation had just enough money in the
kitty to buy a new Bible for the parish
church. However, the town bear suddenly
died, leaving the town facing something of a
dilemma. With only enough cash to buy
either the Bible or a new bear, the choice
was simple: a new bear.

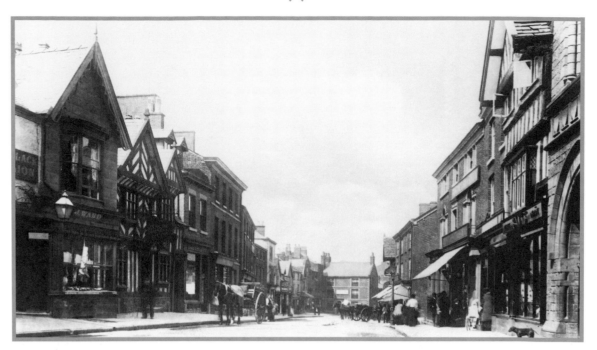

CONGLETON, HIGH STREET 1903 49476
A few half-timbered buildings still survive, including the 15th century Swan and Lion. Others include the White Lion Hotel and the Bear's Head Hotel.

CONGLETON, THE OLD MILL 1902 48675
The first silk mill in England had been established at Derby by John Lombe in 1715. Lombe had worked as a silk weaver in Italy where he secretly made drawings of the machinery. He returned to England and opened his factory. It is believed that he was the victim of a contract killing arranged by the Italians.

CONGLETON, DANE VALLEY BRIDGE 1898 42175
The Macclesfield Canal was not completed until 1831, but provided a link between the Peak Forest and the Trent & Mersey canals. It came into railway ownership in 1846, and continued to attract traffic. The main problem was that its width and depth prevented its reaching its full potential.

ASTBURY, THE VILLAGE AND THE CHURCH 1902 48663
The ivy-clad cottages facing the village green were built in the 19th century for agricultural workers, and are an example of the general improvement in housing for estate workers. By 1871 there were 23,720 freeholders in the county, but the vast majority owned less than one acre.

CONGLETON, MORETON OLD HALL 1902 48670
Two miles south of Congleton stands Little Moreton Hall, a magnificent moated manor house, originally built in the mid-15th century by Sir Richard de Moreton and added to by successive generations of his family. As with many houses of this period there is a secret room; the difference at Little Moreton is that a second secret room exists. It is beneath the moat.

GAWSWORTH, THE CHURCH 1897 40461

Gawsworth Church dates mainly from the 15th century. In the chancel are the tombs of some of the Fytton family, including Sir Edward (1550-1606) who became Lord President of Munster, and Mary Fytton who was a maid of honour to Elizabeth I, but was soon disgraced following an affair with the Earl of Pembroke. She is also one of the contenders as the Dark Lady of Shakespeare's sonnets.

GAWSWORTH, GAWSWORTH HALL 1898 42610

Gawsworth's new hall was built in the 18th century by Lord Mohun. In November 1711 Lord Mohun fought a duel in Hyde Park against the Duke of Hamilton, in which both men were killed. It was not Mohun's first duel. He had fought and killed at the age of seventeen, and had been tried for murder and acquitted by his peers.

Macclesfield
Park Green 1903 49465

On 15 August 1819, Henry Hunt, a leading advocate for
Parliamentary reform, stopped here on his way to address a
meeting in Manchester. Macclesfield had already sent a petition
to the Commons signed by over two-thirds of the male
population. Some local men went with Hunt to Manchester, but
there is no record of their being killed or injured in the ensuing
Peterloo Massacre.

MACCLESFIELD, PARK GREEN 1897 42597

It was here and on the Market Place that local people met to protest about unemployment and hardship in the years following the defeat of Napoleon. In March 1817 the remnants of the Blanketeers arrived in the town, having been dispersed by cavalry at Stockport. Once again cavalry were waiting for them and only a handful escaped towards Leek.

MACCLESFIELD, THE TOWN HALL 1897 40440

The Town Hall was enlarged in 1869 at a cost of £15,200, and many locals considered the expense to be a waste of money; there were more important things to spend it on than councillors full of their own self importance. The work included a new council chamber, the old one being converted into committee rooms, and a new facade complete with Ionic columns.

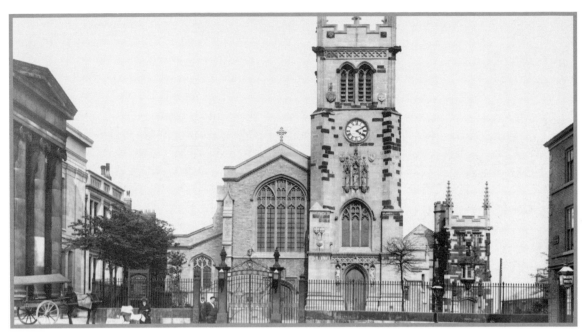

MACCLESFIELD, THE PARISH CHURCH 1903 49456

The parish church was founded in 1278 by Queen Eleanor and dedicated to All Hallows (All Saints). Rebuilt in 1739, and again between 1898 and 1901, the church was at some time in the 18th century rededicated to St Michael and All Angels.

MACCLESFIELD, CHESTERGATE 1898 42600

Along with Mill Street and Jordangate, Chestergate was one of the first streets to be properly paved, and, more importantly, to be provided with surface drainage. Until 1825 there were no surface drains in Macclesfield and the only part of the town with a piped water supply was the area around the Market Place.

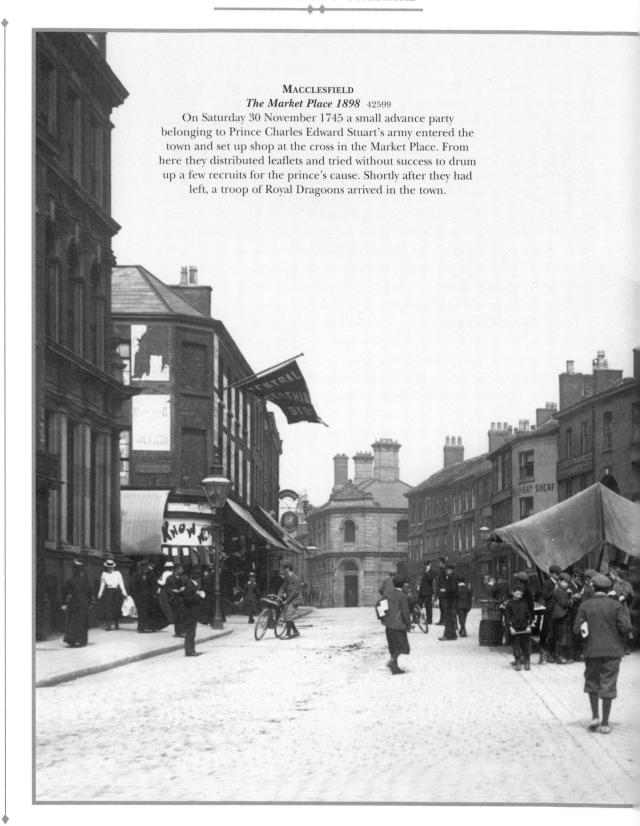

MACCLESFIELD
The Market Place 1898 42599
On Saturday 30 November 1745 a small advance party
belonging to Prince Charles Edward Stuart's army entered the
town and set up shop at the cross in the Market Place. From
here they distributed leaflets and tried without success to drum
up a few recruits for the prince's cause. Shortly after they had
left, a troop of Royal Dragoons arrived in the town.

MACCLESFIELD, THE BARRACKS 1903 49470

On 30 November 1745 a troop of the Royal Dragoons arrived in the town and were billeted overnight. The following morning the officer was telling the Mayoress that he and his men would protect her, when news came of the imminent arrival of Prince Charles Edward and his army. It was said that the dragoons left town in as much haste as did the Mayoress.

MACCLESFIELD, THE SUNDAY SCHOOL 1897 40460

Sunday schools were where most children received a rudimentary education until the passing of Forster's Education Act. By 1812 the schools run by John Whittaker had over 2,000 children enrolled, and ideally Whittaker needed one large building to house them all. Thanks to donations the Large Sunday School, as it was then known, opened in April 1814.

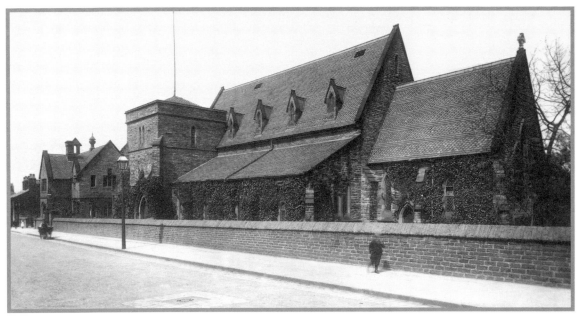

MACCLESFIELD, ST PETER'S CHURCH 1903 49460

MACCLESFIELD
St Peter's Church 1903

Built in 1848 with funds raised almost entirely from public subscriptions, St Peter's was consecrated in July 1849 by the Bishop of Chester, Dr Graham. One of the church's distinguishing features was the high-pitched roof covered with ornamental Staffordshire tiles. This photograph was taken a few years prior to the tower being heightened so that it could accommodate a clock and a belfry.

MACCLESFIELD
The Free Library 1903

Built in the Victorian Gothic style, the Public Library opened in 1876. It was built at the expense of local MP David Chadwick, who also paid for the initial stock of 10,000 books. There were several other libraries in the town, such as the Macclesfield Equitable Provident Society and the Useful Knowledge Society, but they tended to cater for specific groups rather than the general public.

MACCLESFIELD, THE FREE LIBRARY 1903 49466

MACCLESFIELD, THE INFIRMARY 1897 40444

Joseph Tunnicliffe, a wealthy silk manufacturer, had been persuaded after some difficulty to make a bequest in favour of an infirmary. However, after Joseph died, it took ten years of legal wrangling before the money (£30,000) was handed over. The site purchased lacked road access and surrounding landowners refused to sell, so the Corporation simply ignored protests and built a road anyway.

MACCLESFIELD, THE PARISH CHURCH c1955 M2021

This photograph shows the Central Station to the right. Opened to passenger traffic in July 1873, on the Bollington/ Marple route, it was rebuilt in 1960. Its reopening was timed to coincide with the closure of the town's other station at Hibel Road.

MACCLESFIELD
West Park 1903
Opened in October 1854, the park covered around sixteen acres, eight of which comprised the old Town Field; the remainder was purchased from an adjoining estate. The park was dedicated to Robert Peel, but hardly anyone ever referred to it as Peel Park. It was later known as West Park, in order to distinguish it from South Park.

◆

MACCLESFIELD
View from Buxton Road c1955
This view shows the high, bleak, windswept road from Macclesfield. There was once a proposal to link Buxton and Macclesfield by light railway, by a route following the road. The railway would have almost certainly used electric traction, something akin to the Manx Electric Tramway.

MACCLESFIELD, WEST PARK 1903 49467

MACCLESFIELD, VIEW FROM BUXTON ROAD c1955 M2037

MACCLESFIELD, THE CAT AND FIDDLE c1955 M2033

MACCLESFIELD
The Cat and Fiddle c1955

The Cat and Fiddle pub is one of the highest in England. From here on a clear day the view could be spectacular: the Cheshire Plain with the Mersey beyond. In the 1880s, it was claimed that it was possible to see Snowdon; but if so, the viewer would have needed a high-powered telescope to distinguish it from the Glyders, which lie on the same line of sight.

POTT SHRIGLEY
The Village c1955

The village of Pott Shrigley, along with places like Whaley and Disley, was in medieval times situated within Macclesfield forest. The settlement was founded at some time during the mid-13th to early 14th century, and by 1492 it even had a school and a library.

POTT SHRIGLEY, THE VILLAGE c1955 B519024

BOLLINGTON, GENERAL VIEW 1897 40478

By the 1860s Bollington was thriving, but during the American Civil War the cotton towns of Lancashire, east Cheshire and north Derbyshire felt the effects of the Federal blockade of Confederate ports. Cotton workers experienced months of hardship and many were forced to seek parish relief. When this picture was taken there would still have been people in Bollington who remembered the cotton famine.

BOLLINGTON, THE CANAL c1955 B519005

Bollington's skyline was and still is dominated by great mills and tall chimneys. The Adelphi, the Waterhouse, and the Clarence are all names to conjure with. Few now serve their original purpose and some have been converted to other uses. The Adelphi Mill in Grimshawe Lane now houses a hotel whilst the remainder of the building has been divided up for use by a large number of businesses.

BOLLINGTON
The Wesleyan Chapel 1897 40480
For some reason best left to the Frith cameraman, one
of Bollington's more interesting structures is in fact just
off camera to the left. There are any number of pictures
of the mills in the archive, but not a single one of the
twenty-three arched railway viaduct straddling the valley
of the Bollin.

BOLLINGTON, GENERAL VIEW 1903 49473
The sight of a man setting up a large tripod camera seemed to fascinate children: hundreds of pictures in the Frith archive seem to point to this. It was no different here at Bollington on a sunny afternoon.

BOLLINGTON, FROM WHITE NANCY c1955 B519009
White Nancy is a tower situated on the ridge to the south of the town, and is said to have been built by a member of the Gaskell family to commemorate the Battle of Waterloo, and to be named after one of the ladies of the family who was named Nancy.

PRESTBURY, HIGH STREET 1896 37439
The tower of St Peter's can just be seen above the roofs on the right-hand side of the picture. In the churchyard lies the grave of Maria Rathbone, a little girl who died having lost her way home and whose body was recovered several weeks later as the result of a dream by a stranger.

PRESTBURY
The Village 1896 37438
On the right is the half-timbered Priest's House, which is thought to date
from the 14th century. Above the entrance is a gallery, and it was from
here that a parson, ejected from the church by the Commonwealth, used
to preach to the villagers. The house later became a bank.

PRESTBURY, THE NORMAN CHAPEL 1896 37443

Restoration work was carried out during the 18th century when a new roof was added. The doorway is one of the oldest in Cheshire, and is famous for the zigzag patterns and beaked heads carved on the arch.

RAINOW, GENERAL VIEW c1955 R307007

The parish of Rainow and Saltersford was one of the most extensive in the whole of Cheshire. One of the more unusual stories in Saltersford's history occurred during the Great War, when the area was invaded by millions of caterpillars. Theories abounded as to how the plague had occurred. Some said it was a plot by the Hun, and that the caterpillars had been dropped by Zeppelin.

RAINOW, THE RISING SUN c1955 R307004

RAINOW
The Rising Sun c1955
It might be interesting to speculate if Paul Mason ever drank here. Paul died in 1752 at the ripe old age of 95, and was the father and grandfather of no less than 94 children.

◆

RAINOW
The Village c1955
The area then had five shops including a post office. There were two schools in Rainow, one Church of England, the other Methodist. As with all agricultural areas, it was common practise for children to work on their family farms before coming to school in the morning and on returning home in the afternoon.

RAINOW, THE VILLAGE c1955 R307005

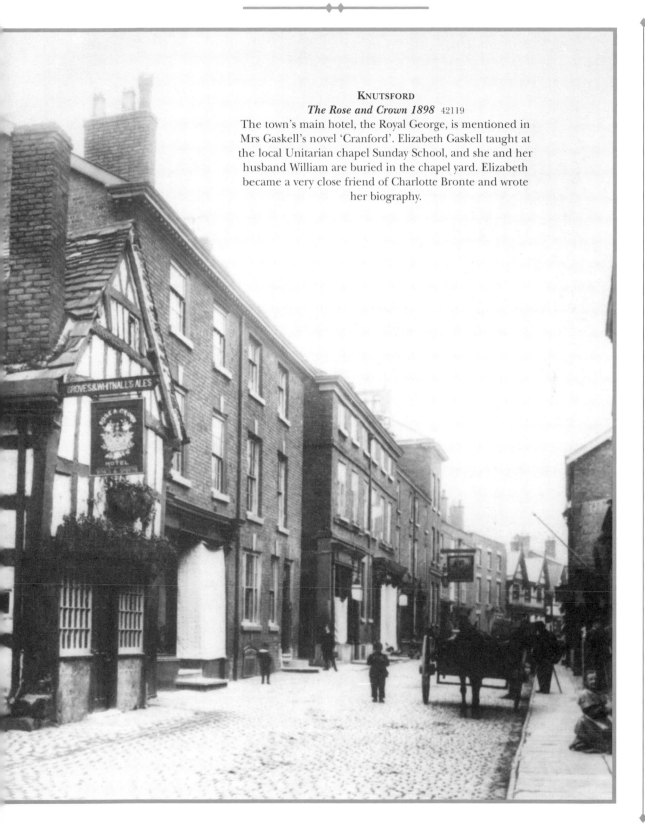

KNUTSFORD
The Rose and Crown 1898 42119

The town's main hotel, the Royal George, is mentioned in Mrs Gaskell's novel 'Cranford'. Elizabeth Gaskell taught at the local Unitarian chapel Sunday School, and she and her husband William are buried in the chapel yard. Elizabeth became a very close friend of Charlotte Bronte and wrote her biography.

KNUTSFORD, TOFT ROAD 1900 45428

Judging by the state of the road, rose growing did not appear to be high on the natives' list of priorities. During the summer every town in the country faced the problem of combating the stench of horse droppings; large cities had to dispose of tons of the stuff every day. It took 7,000 gallons of water to cleanse one mile of roadway, 18 feet in width, at a cost of 8s 4d a mile.

ALDERLEY EDGE, THE RAILWAY STATION 1896 37446

Originally named Alderley, the station became Alderley & Chorley in April 1853, and Alderley Edge in January 1876. The station closed to goods traffic on 30 November 1964; both Wilmslow and Chelford closed for goods on 4 May 1970; Styal in 1963; and Handforth in 1958. Heavy use of these stations by commuters has ensured their remaining open.

ALDERLEY EDGE, GENERAL VIEW 1896 37445
A view from the railway station which shows the residential nature of the place. It was once said that there were more millionaires living in Alderley Edge than anywhere else in England, save for London itself.

ALDERLEY EDGE, THE OLD MILL 1896 37478

ALDERLEY EDGE
The Old Mill 1896
The old mill dates from the 15th century. What is thought to be the oldest inhabited house in Cheshire is also near Alderley Edge: the stone-built portion of Chorley Hall is thought to date from about 1330, the remainder being Elizabethan.

◆

ALDERLEY EDGE
London Road 1896
The residential nature of the place led to the establishment of quality retail outlets. A number of retailers and farmers had produce rounds in Alderley, delivering groceries, dairy produce and even wines and spirits to the door, or rather, the back door. Quality was the name of the game, and value for money was given, as advance orders were usually placed on the next delivery.

ALDERLEY EDGE, LONDON ROAD 1896 37447

ALDERLEY EDGE, THE EDGE AND HAUGH 1896 37462
The Edge is not the highest point in the county; at the eastern border with Derbyshire the land rises to nearly
1800ft, and to over 1900ft at Black Hill in Longdendale.

ALDERLEY EDGE, THE HOLY WELL 1896 37469
In medieval times each holy well was believed to be protected by a saint, and many were named accordingly, e.g.
St Anne's Well. The revenues from these wells could be substantial; the faithful had to pay to take the waters.
During the Dissolution they were closed on the orders of Thomas Cromwell, Chief Minister to Henry VIII, in an
attempt to destroy any cult following that might exist.

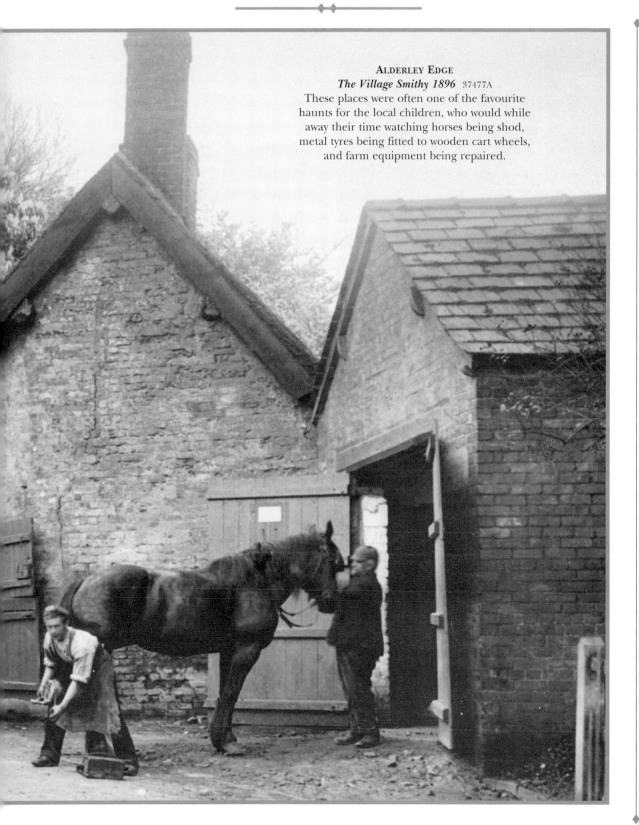

ALDERLEY EDGE
The Village Smithy 1896 37477A
These places were often one of the favourite
haunts for the local children, who would while
away their time watching horses being shod,
metal tyres being fitted to wooden cart wheels,
and farm equipment being repaired.

WILMSLOW, POWNELL HALL 1897 39615
When this picture of Pownell Hall was taken, it had been acquired by Henry Boddington, a member of the Manchester brewing family. Boddington spent a vast amount on Pownell, transforming it into one of the finest examples of Arts and Crafts Movement decoration in the county.

WILMSLOW, GROVE STREET 1897 39604
When this picture was taken much of the town was fairly new, having been built over the previous thirty years or so to meet the demand for housing from Stockport and Manchester-based business people wishing to live in more rural surroundings.

WILMSLOW, STATION ROAD 1897 39606

With Manchester so close, Wilmslow was one of the early centres of nonconformism in east Cheshire; others included Congleton, Macclesfield and Knutsford.

HALE, MAIN STREET 1907 58620

Hale is a typical example of a suburban post office in the Edwardian era. Housed in Kennerley's drapery store, local mail would be sorted and delivered from here. There was even a delivery on Christmas Day. Letters and parcels for other destinations would be collected by horse-drawn van and taken to the nearest general post office for sorting.

HALE, ASHLEY ROAD 1913 66067

ALTRINCHAM, THE MARKET PLACE 1897 39063

HALE
Ashley Road 1913
A motor car rattles along Ashley Road. In those days the nearest AA recommended hotel was the Unicorn at Altrincham, a fourteen-bed establishment with garaging for two automobiles. The telephone number of the hotel was 1436, which indicates that an extensive telephone network already existed in the town.

◆

ALTRINCHAM
The Market Place 1897
Cabs await their next customers. To take a cab from here to St Anne's Square in Manchester cost 9d per mile for one or two people, and a 1s a mile for three or four people.

ALTRINCHAM, OLD HOUSES 1903 49669
These old thatched cottages were still standing in 1903. The town is ancient, having been granted borough status in 1290 by the Lord of the Manor Hamon de Massey. By 1903, the population stood at around 16,800 and, by 1920, would grow by another 1,000 or so.

ALTRINCHAM
Stamford New Road 1907 58622
An electric tramcar trundles along
Stamford New Road. At its height
the tramway systems serving
Manchester and the surrounding
area operated over 300 route miles.

ESTATE
OFFICES

STYAL, QUARRY BANK MILL 1897 39616
Samuel Greg's Quarry Bank Mill stands on the banks of the Bollin where it flows through a wooded glen. Originally water-powered, the mill remains intact, and is now in the care of the National Trust. The waterwheel is long gone, though the sluices can still be seen.

STYAL, THE VILLAGE c1955 39617
The Greg family lived nearby at Norcliffe Hall, which was built in the Elizabethan style. The village was laid out from 1790 by mill owner Samuel Greg to house his mill workers, and was one of a number built in east Cheshire by industrialists.

LYMM, THE CANAL c1960 L122054
The Bridgewater Canal. A pair of Horsfield's narrow boats make their way through Lymm with a cargo of coal. The motorized narrow boat is towing an old, formerly horse-drawn butty.

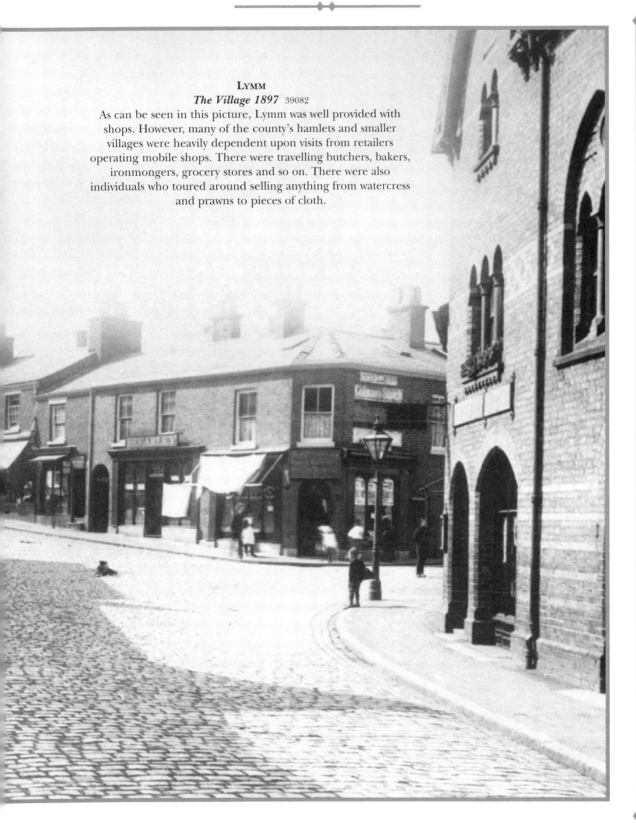

LYMM
The Village 1897 39082
As can be seen in this picture, Lymm was well provided with
shops. However, many of the county's hamlets and smaller
villages were heavily dependent upon visits from retailers
operating mobile shops. There were travelling butchers, bakers,
ironmongers, grocery stores and so on. There were also
individuals who toured around selling anything from watercress
and prawns to pieces of cloth.

LYMM, THE CROSS 1897 40483

The 17th century cross and village stocks. Local man Henry Daniels introduced fustian cutting to Lymm, having first gone to Manchester to learn the business. The pieces (rolls) were delivered by canal boat, and after cutting were returned to Manchester for dyeing and finishing.

WARRINGTON, CHURCH STREET 1894 33805

At this time the annual event known as Walking Day was still practiced. Every year, children from the town's churches, chapels, and Sunday schools dressed in white and paraded through the streets. The custom survived until recent times.

WARRINGTON, BUTTERWALK 1894 33806
This photograph shows Joseph Beswick's Ye Old Fox Tobacco Stores.

WARRINGTON, BRIDGE STREET c1955 W29060
Woodhouse's store has recently opened in what was previously Singleton's; the shop received a new frontage and complete refit. It was also in Bridge Street that John Howard lodged when printing his work on prison reform.

WARRINGTON, THE TOWN HALL, NEW GATES 1895 36688
These ornamental gates had only recently been erected when this picture was taken. Probably the most interesting monument in the town is the altar tomb of Sir John and Lady Butler who were murdered in 1463. One of the effigies is of their black servant, who managed to save the life of the murdered couple's infant son.

WARRINGTON, THE SWING BRIDGE c1960 W29056
Whenever the Chester Road and Northwich Road swing-bridges are opened to allow ships to pass along the Manchester Ship Canal, Warrington grinds to a halt; traffic tails back for hundreds of yards either side. When this picture was taken, things weren't so bad. In the background is the Latchford high-level road-bridge.

GRAPPENHALL
The Canal c1955

The Knutsford Road swing-bridge lies open to allow the passage of a ship outward-bound from Manchester. In the background is the Latchford railway viaduct, constructed in 1893. For several months after its completion the viaduct was used for freight trains, with only the original line being retained for passenger traffic.

◆

NEW BRIGHTON
The Pier and Parade 1892

In 1830 a retired builder from Everton, James Atherton, bought 170 acres of sandhills on the northern tip of the Wirral, with the aim of creating a new seaside resort to rival Brighton. When the town was first laid out it was to be an exclusive place, but within a few years, cheap, terraced houses had been built and Atherton's vision was in tatters.

GRAPPENHALL, THE CANAL C1955 G200001

NEW BRIGHTON, THE PIER AND PARADE 1892 30416

NEW BRIGHTON
The Beach 1887 20067
Though the photographers' stalls were harmless enough, the
beach by this date had acquired a reputation for cheap and tacky
sideshows, gambling, brawling and drunkenness. In the
background is Fort Perch Rock. Local fishermen could always
earn their beer money after the fort had fired off a few practice
shots by salvaging the cannon balls and selling them back
to the army.

NEW BRIGHTON, THE TOWER AND SANDS 1900 45163
Based on Blackpool Tower, New Brighton' tower was built between 1897 and 1900 at a cost of £120,000. At 621ft, it was much higher than Blackpool's, and was the tallest structure in Britain.Its life was somewhat short. Neglected throughout the Great War, it was declared unsafe in 1918, and was demolished the following year.

NEW BRIGHTON
General View 1892

The town is already heading down market and away from James Atherton's ideals. Cheap and tatty eating houses dominated Aquarium Parade to such an extent that it was known better as Ham and Eggs Parade. In 1905 the Corporation succeeded in buying the Parade and immediately demolished it.

WALLASEY
High Street c1960

In 1801 the village of Wallasey had 663 inhabitants. By 1851 the number had risen to 8,339, and by 1951 it was 101,369, making Wallasey the third largest town in Cheshire.

NEW BRIGHTON, GENERAL VIEW 1892 30418

WALLASEY, HIGH STREET c1960 W164063

WALLASEY, THE CHURCH AND TOWER C1873 8468

St Hilary's is one of only eight churches in the country dedicated to the saint. The lone tower dates back to the rebuilding of the 1530s, the rest of the church having been demolished in 1760. The church in the background was rebuilt in 1858-59 after the previous one had been destroyed by fire.

WALLASEY, THE VILLAGE C1965 W164082

This photograph shows the old village centre of Wallasey.

EGREMONT, KING STREET 1912 64429

A tram rattles down the street. Both Birkenhead and Wallasey Corporations operated their own tramway systems. Birkenhead's was electrified in 1901 and ran until 1937; Wallasey's operated from 1902 to 1933.

EGREMONT, THE LANDING STAGE 1890 24427

John Askew, who was at one time Liverpool's harbour master, founded the Egremont ferry service. The service finally closed in 1941 after the pier was badly damaged when a ship collided with it.

EGREMONT, THE FERRY BOAT 1912 64443

Until 1817 the Mersey ferry service was erratic and subject to the vagaries of wind, tides and weather. In that year the paddle ferry 'Etna' began a regular service between Queen's Dock, Liverpool and Tranmere.

EGREMONT, THE PROMENADE 1902 48662

Egremont was planned by developer John Askew, a former slave-trader who made his money on land deals involving Liverpool Corporation's unwanted properties in the Wirral. At first he built himself a house which he named Egremont, after his home town in Cumbria, and the name spread from there.

BIRKENHEAD, THE DOCKS c1965 B399036

BIRKENHEAD
The Docks c1965
The original plan for the docks involved building a wall across the mouth of Wallasey Pool to create a tidal dock, or float. Though the Morpeth and Egerton Docks were completed in the 1840s, work on the Great Float was not started until Birkenhead and Liverpool Docks were merged under the Mersey Docks & Harbour Board.

— ◆

BIRKENHEAD
Hamilton Square and City Hall c1965
Hamilton Square was laid out in 1826 by Gillespie Graham on the lines of an Edinburgh square. The Town Hall was modelled on that at Bolton, and was completed in 1883, though it was damaged by fire in 1901.

BIRKENHEAD, HAMILTON SQUARE AND CITY HALL c1965 B399041

BIRKENHEAD, WOODCHURCH ROAD 1954 B399002

This photograph shows a typical pre-supermarket scene. Along here were branches of both national and Cheshire retailers including Dewhurst, the butchers, and Waterworths.

PORT SUNLIGHT, POST OFFICE CORNER c1960 P188066

The earlier houses built at Port Sunlight were a mixture of styles. The village had a pub, the Bridge Inn, which was designed to look like an old coaching inn, but opened as a temperance hotel. Lever allowed villagers a vote about a licence. They were in favour of beer sales and Lever, though a staunch teetotaller, went along with the result.

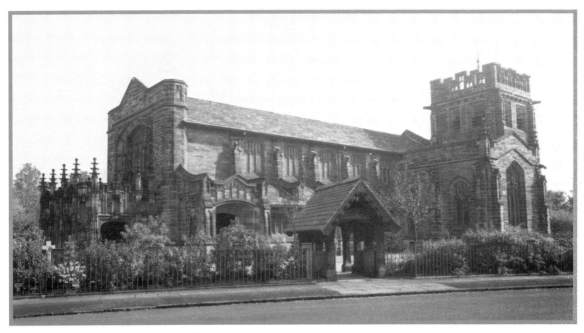

PORT SUNLIGHT, CHRIST CHURCH c1960 P188053
Christ Church is where Lord Leverhulme and his wife, Elizabeth, are buried, as well as their son, the 2nd Viscount, and his wife. The church is known for its bronze effigies by William Gascombe, who also designed the village war memorial.

HALTON, THE CASTLE 1900 45439
Along with Frodsham, Halton was of strategic importance. These castles commanded the southern shore of the Mersey estuary and controlled vital river crossing points at Runcorn and Hale.

RUNCORN, WESTON POINT c1955 R67019

Since the 1820s Runcorn has been a centre for the chemical industry, with factories producing a wide range of products. In 1803, John Johnson opened a small soap factory; within thirty years Johnson Brothers were manufacturing 36 per cent of the country's soap and had diversified into coal and chemicals.

RUNCORN, BIG POOL 1923 73906

One hundred years earlier Runcorn was already linked to Liverpool by a steam river packet service which operated two sailings every day from George's Dock. The Lady Stanley sailed every day from the south end of the Parade to Weston Point.

RUNCORN, THE DOCKS c1900 R67301

One of the oldest cargoes handled here was china clay from Cornwall destined for the Potteries. In the 18th century the clay was transferred to river craft to go via the Weaver Navigation to Winsford, and then went on by road. With the opening of the canal system it was possible to trans-ship at Runcorn directly into narrow boats, and for the clay to be taken direct to the Potteries.

RUNCORN
The Transporter Bridge 1899 43432A
The transporter bridge connected
Runcorn with Widnes on the north
shore. The transporter remained in use
until 1961, when it was replaced by a
road bridge.

RUNCORN, THE RAILWAY VIADUCT 1900 45433

The London & North Western Railway viaduct over the Mersey. Work began in 1864 to construct a line from Weaver Junction to provide the LNWR with a more direct route from London and Crewe to Liverpool.

RUNCORN, THE TWO BRIDGES 1929 82384

The transporter bridge and the railway viaduct. In this picture we see the Manchester Ship Canal with the Mersey immediately beyond it. We can also see how the transporter sat in relation to the Ship Canal, and that it was essential for the transporter operator to keep a sharp look-out for shipping in order to avoid a collision.

RUNCORN, THE SWING BRIDGE AND CANAL 1900 45435
There were nine swing bridges over the canal, seven of them being where major roads crossed. Some crossing points not considered important enough for a bridge were provided with ferries. Some ferries were nothing more than rowing boats, while a few could carry one horse-drawn vehicle.

RUNCORN, WIDNES BRIDGE c1955 R67043
The new single-span 1,082ft road-bridge built between the railway viaduct and the transporter. Once the bridge opened the transporter, which was one of only three in the country, was decommissioned.

RUNCORN, DEVONSHIRE PLACE c1955 R67044

RUNCORN
Devonshire Place c1955
In 1964 Runcorn New Town was designated, the aim being to increase the population from 29,000 to 100,000. The development included the construction of Shopping City, which at the time was one of the largest retail centres in the country.

RUNCORN
Top Locks c1955
Runcorn is now the terminus of the Bridgewater Canal, but there was a time when it continued down a massive flight of locks to connect with the Mersey and the Ship Canal. There were two flights, side-by-side. One set was closed in 1949, the other was abandoned and filled-in, in 1966, after several years of neglect.

RUNCORN, TOP LOCKS c1955 R67001

NORTHWICH, THE SWING BRIDGE 1900 45421

The River Weaver. As well as for exporting salt, the Weaver was used to bring coal to Winsford, Northwich and Winnington. In the early years china clay was brought by barge to Winsford, where it was trans-shipped into horse-drawn wagons and taken by road to the Potteries.

NORTHWICH, THE ANDERTON BOAT LIFT c1960 N43026

The Anderton Boat Lift at Northwich was built in 1875, providing a link between the Weaver Navigation and the Trent & Mersey Canal. Designed by Leader Williams, it comprised two water-tight tanks, each capable of holding a pair of narrow boats. The Trent & Mersey was connected to the upper level by means of a 162ft wrought-iron aqueduct; the Weaver was connected by a small basin.

NORTHWICH, THE SWING BRIDGE 1900 45422
The Weaver Navigation prospered throughout the 19th century owing to a very active policy of continuous upgrading and modernization programmes that included deepening the river, widening the channel, reducing the number of locks and enlarging those that remained. Today, coasters with a deadweight capacity of up to 1,000 tonnes can navigate the Weaver.

NORTHWICH, CROOKED HOUSES 1903 49673

The mining of salt led to many buildings suffering the effects of subsidence; one of the more spectacular episodes involved The Witch and Barrel pub sinking one Saturday night into a big hole.

NORTHWICH, THE BULL RING 1903 49678

Within a few years the Bull Ring became one of those places where pedestrians took their lives in their hands, having to dodge scores of ICI workers as they freewheeled four, five, even six abreast down Winnington Hill, through the Bull Ring and over Town Bridge.

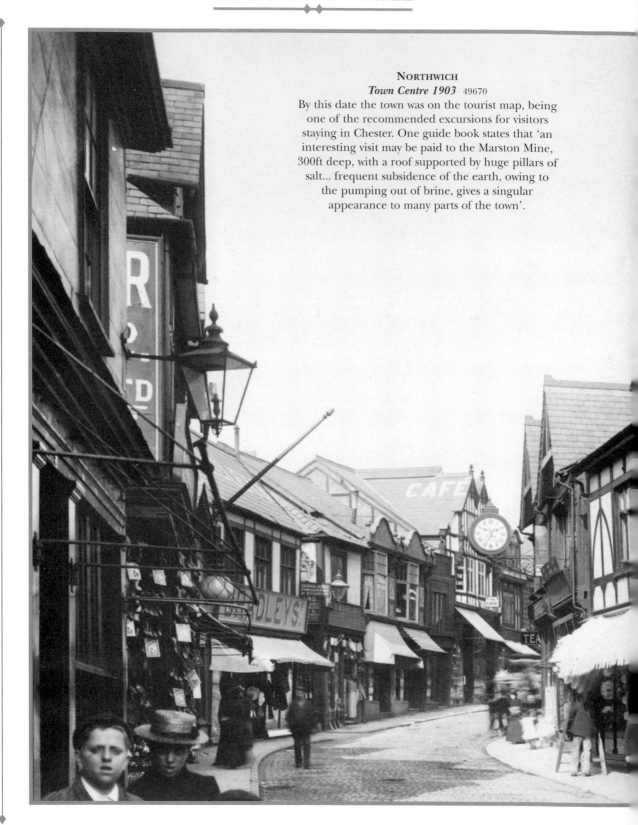

NORTHWICH
Town Centre 1903 49670
By this date the town was on the tourist map, being one of the recommended excursions for visitors staying in Chester. One guide book states that 'an interesting visit may be paid to the Marston Mine, 300ft deep, with a roof supported by huge pillars of salt... frequent subsidence of the earth, owing to the pumping out of brine, gives a singular appearance to many parts of the town'.

NORTHWICH, HIGH STREET 1903 49671

At this time the town's population stood at about 17,000, while that of Nantwich was somewhere between 7,500 and 8,000. Market day was on a Friday, with half-day closing being observed on a Wednesday.

WINSFORD, WARTON HILL c1955 W561004

Winsford High Street boasted an outlet of the Zan chain of ironmongers. The company had around sixteen stores throughout Cheshire, and also operated a fleet of mobile shops which toured the rural areas.

NANTWICH
Welsh Row 1898
In the distance is the tower of St Mary's, founded shortly after the Norman Conquest but almost totally rebuilt in the 14th and 15th centuries thanks to endowments from local salt merchants. The church was heavily restored in 1885.

◆

NANTWICH
High Street 1898
In 1584 much of the town was destroyed by fire. Rebuilding has left Nantwich with a number of late-Tudor buildings, one of the most interesting of which is the Crown Hotel. The hotel is a three-story, half-timbered structure noted for the compartmentalized design of its timbering.

NANTWICH, WELSH ROW 1898 42181

NANTWICH, HIGH STREET 1898 42179

NANTWICH, HIGH STREET c1965 N3060
In this picture we get some idea of the architectural diversity of the town centre. Genuine Elizabethan and 19th-century Tudor-revival buildings rub shoulders with Georgian hotels and modern shop fronts.

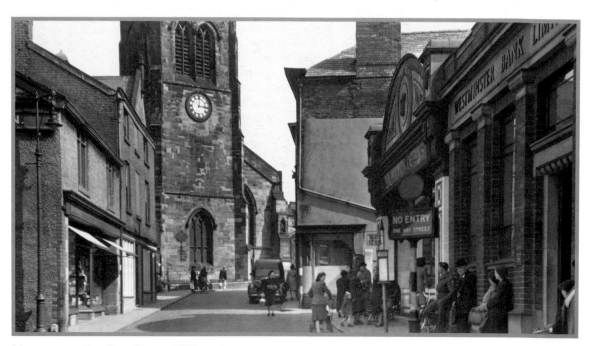

MIDDLEWICH, THE BULL RING c1955 M237001
The salt industry both here and at Nantwich suffered as a result of the shelving of a scheme to open the rivers of these towns to navigation. Consequently, salt from Nantwich and Middlewich attracted higher transport costs than that from Northwich.

CHESTER, STANLEY PALACE 1923 73867
In 1828 the Earl of Derby presented the city with Stanley Palace. Built in 1591 for Peter Warburton, MP for Chester, this fine town house passed into the hands of the Stanley family through the marriage of his daughter to Sir Thomas Stanley.

CHESTER, WATERGATE ROWS 1888 20611

These galleries are unique to Chester, and are known to have existed in the 13th century. Opinion is divided as to their origins. One theory is that they might well be an echo of the Roman pattern of domestic building: a combination of apartments, workshops, and shops which were the Roman equivalent of fast-food outlets.

CHESTER, WATERGATE STREET 1895 36453

Watergate Street is said to contain three of the finest examples of half-timber buildings still standing. Bishop Lloyd's House dates from 1615 and God's Provident House from 1652, though the latter was rebuilt in 1892 in the traditional style, using many original timbers. The third and oldest of the buildings is Stanley Palace.

CHESTER, EASTGATE STREET 1895 36447
The neo-classical building with four columns was built by George Williams in 1860, and just beyond it is one of the smaller Victorian half-timbered buildings. Note the tram lines. Eastgate simply wasn't wide enough for two tracks, so the line is single with passing loops.

CHESTER
Eastgate 1903 49887
Foregate Street looking towards the Eastgate. The clock was presented to the city by Edward Evans-Lloyd in 1897 to commemorate Queen Victoria's diamond jubilee. The clock was made by J B Joyce of Whitchurch and sits on top of ornate ironwork designed by John Douglas.

CHESTER, EASTGATE STREET 1929 82746
The gate was built in the late 1760s, paid for by Lord Grosvenor. On the right of the picture we have an example of twentieth century half-timber revival.

CHESTER, THE CROSS 1903 49881
The corner of Eastgate Street and Bridge Street. The buildings are from the Victorian half-timber revival period, designed by T M Lockwood in 1888. This area of the city is known as The Cross. Until it was demolished during the Civil War, a medieval cross stood nearby. The Cross was restored to its original site in 1975.

CHESTER, BRIDGE STREET 1903 49889

This was the year the Corporation tramway changed over to electric traction. On race days the busiest route on the tramway was that to Saltney. With the Roodee Racecourse situated halfway along it, trams carried racegoers in vast numbers from both Chester and Saltney stations.

CHESTER, OLD MANSIONS ON BRIDGE STREET 1895 36445

Here we see an excellent view of the Row. Bridge Street, Eastgate Street and Watergate Street have Rows on either side. The only other place in Europe with a similar type of arrangement is Thun, in Switzerland.

CHESTER
Bridge Street 1888
Lower Bridge Street included a number of interesting buildings. The Old King's Head dates from the early 17th century, as does The Falcon (1626). The latter is where Handel stayed when he visited the city in 1741.

◆

CHESTER
Bridge Street 1888
The Bear and Billet public house in Lower Bridge Street was built in 1664. At some time during the 19th century the pub frontage has been modified so that there are continuous windows on two floors.

CHESTER, BRIDGE STREET 1888 20600

CHESTER, BRIDGE STREET 1888 20601

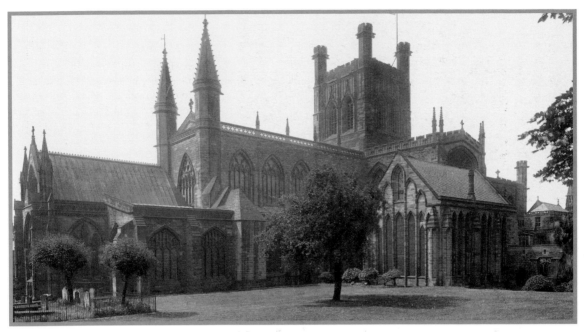

CHESTER, THE CATHEDRAL 1923 73837
Built of red sandstone, Chester cathedral was founded in 1092 as a Benedictine abbey. The present buildings date from the 13th to the 16th centuries, though some earlier Norman features survive. At the Dissolution the building was saved from destruction when it was chosen as the cathedral for the newly formed diocese of Chester.

CHESTER, NORTHGATE 1903 49882
In Anglo-Saxon times a church dedicated to St Werburgh stood on part of the site now occupied by the cathedral. St Werburgh was a daughter of King Wulfhere of Mercia. Werburgh was supervisor of all the nunneries in Mercia and died at Trentham in AD699. In AD874 St Werburgh's remains were transferred to Chester to prevent them from falling into the hands of Danish invaders.

CHESTER, THE PHOENIX TOWER 1888 20618
It was from here, on 24 September 1645, that King Charles watched the Battle of Rowton Heath, which took place just outside the city walls. It was a chaotic affair in which one of the last Royalist armies capable of taking to the field was destroyed.

CHESTER, THE CATHEDRAL 1923 73860

The great Norman undercroft of Chester Cathedral. As well as its more ancient parts, Chester has the distinction of being the only cathedral since the 15th century to have a detached bell tower built. The Addleshaw Tower was completed in 1974, its construction deemed necessary owing to the unsafe condition of the bell-frame in the central tower.

CHESTER, THE SUSPENSION BRIDGE 1888 20627

In 1852 a suspension bridge was built over the Dee to link the suburb of Queen's Park with the Groves on the north side of the river. The bridge was rebuilt in 1923.

CHESTER, ST MARY'S CHURCH 1906 55280
Looking across the river to the suburb of Handbridge. Featured is the church of St Mary-without-the-Walls, which was completed in 1887; its distinctive spire is something of a local landmark.

CHESTER, THE BANDSTAND 1914 67544

By the banks of the Dee. Though used by excursion and pleasure craft, the river at Chester was last used commercially in the 1930s when a barge took a cargo of tar from the gasworks to Queensferry. Even so, the city remained the customs port for Rhyl and the Deeside ports, and ships belonging to John Summers & Co were registered at Chester, though it is unlikely that they ever came up the river.

CHESTER, THE GROVES 1923 73875

The newly rebuilt suspension bridge is in the background. At the landing stage a pleasure steamer is about to depart on an afternoon excursion.

CHESTER, DEE BRIDGE 1923 73881

CHESTER
Dee Bridge 1923
There has been a bridge over the river at this point for centuries. The old bridge with its seven irregular arches dates from the late 13th century and was partially rebuilt during the mid-14th century.

◆

CHESTER
The River Dee 1923
The park on the south side of the old Dee bridge is known as Edgar's Field in memory of the Saxon king, Edgar. In AD972 Edgar engaged in a set piece of power politics at Chester, when he was rowed in state along the Dee by eight Celtic kings and chieftains.

CHESTER, THE RIVER DEE 1923 73870

CHESTER, THE RIVER 1891 28891
Hugh Lupus, the first of the Norman earls of Chester, is said to have ordered the construction of a weir so that the mills would have a regular source of water power. There were mills along the banks of the Dee until 1909.

ECCLESTON, THE FERRY c1886 1722
This small steamer might be one of the craft based at Chester for summer excursion work along the Dee, though it is possible that it could be a privately owned craft, as her carrying capacity is somewhat restricted.

ECCLESTON
The Ferry 1895 36454
Eccleston is a few miles up the Dee from Chester.
Here the river charts a more leisurely course as it
makes its way to the sea. This photograph depicts
the chain-operated flat-decked ferry.

CHESTER, EATON HALL 1914 67528

Outside Chester stands Eaton Hall, seat of the Duke of Westminster. Designed by Alfred Waterhouse in grand Victorian Gothic, the hall and estate even had its own railway. The 15-inch gauge line was based on that developed by Sir Arthur Heywood at Duffield Bank near Derby. Much of the hall and the railway has been demolished.

CHOLMONDELEY, THE CASTLE AND PARK 1898 42482

In the 14th century the nearby village of Malpas was under constant threat of attack from the Welsh, and there was an unsuccessful attempt to have the chapel on the Cholmondeley estate raised in status to a church, as it was considered a safer place for worship. Members of the Cholmondeley family are buried in St Oswald's, Malpas.

BEESTON
The Castle 1888

Beeston was one of a series of fortresses built by Rannulf de Blundeville, Earl of Chester and Lincoln. Rannulf died before Beeston was finished, with the result that the domestic buildings were never erected. The castle passed into royal hands, and during the Civil War it withstood a year-long siege before surrendering on 16 November 1645.

◆

CREWE
The Station c1960

In September 1960 the electrification of the London Midland Region's line between Crewe and Manchester was completed. This was followed by the Liverpool-to-Crewe line, and then south to London's Euston. By 1974 the whole of the West Coast main line, north of Crewe to Glasgow, had been converted to AC electrification.

BEESTON, THE CASTLE 1888 20655

CREWE, THE STATION c1960 C316104

CREWE, MARKET STREET c1960 C316032

There was a time when Crewe market was at its busiest after 6.30pm, workers having gone home for a bite to eat before coming out to shop. As with all markets, there was a wide range of goods for sale, including fish, meat, poultry, groceries, carpets, lino, clothing, and even patent medicines and cure-alls.

CREWE. MARKET STREET c1960 C316012

White's 1860 directory listed no less than 38 fairs in the county, including Crewe, where its establishment was probably influenced by the town's extensive railway facilities, making it an ideal centre for the transportation of livestock.

CREWE, EARLE STREET 1951 C316011

It was to the wrought iron railings outside the front entrance of the municipal buildings that relatives of patients in the isolation hospital came for news of their loved ones. Patients suffering from diseases such as scarlet fever or diphtheria were not allowed visitors, and telephone calls to the hospital were not encouraged.

CREWE, THE SQUARE C1960 C316014

The Odeon cinema is typical of the super cinema style of architecture that came into vogue during the 1930s. When redevelopment came, the Odeon survived, but a number of other buildings were demolished. They were replaced by uninspiring, flat-roofed shops of little or no merit. Tarmac replaced cobbles, and drab concrete street lamps got the better of the ornate standards in this picture.

Index

Frith Book Co 1999 Titles

From 2000 we aim at publishing 100 new books each year. For latest catalogue please contact Frith Book Co

Barnstaple	1-85937-084-5	£12.99	Oct 99		Maidstone	1-85937-056-X	£12.99	Sep 99
Blackpool	1-85937-049-7	£12.99	Sep 99		Northumberland & Tyne and Wear	1-85937-072-1	£14.99	Sep 99
Bognor Regis	1-85937-055-1	£12.99	Sep 99		North Yorkshire	1-85937-048-9	£14.99	Sep 99
Bristol	1-85937-050-0	£12.99	Sep 99		Nottingham	1-85937-060-8	£12.99	Sep 99
Cambridge	1-85937-092-6	£12.99	Oct 99		Oxfordshire	1-85937-076-4	£14.99	Oct 99
Cambridgeshire	1-85937-086-1	£14.99	Nov 99		Penzance	1-85937-069-1	£12.99	Sep 99
Cheshire	1-85937-045-4	£14.99	Sep 99		Reading	1-85937-087-X	£12.99	Nov 99
Chester	1-85937-090-X	£12.99	Nov 99		St Ives	1-85937-068-3	£12.99	Sep 99
Chesterfield	1-85937-071-3	£12.99	Sep 99		Salisbury	1-85937-091-8	£12.99	Nov 99
Chichester	1-85937-089-6	£12.99	Nov 99		Scarborough	1-85937-104-3	£12.99	Sep 99
Cornwall	1-85937-054-3	£14.99	Sep 99		Scottish Castles	1-85937-077-2	£14.99	Oct 99
Cotswolds	1-85937-099-3	£14.99	Nov 99		Sevenoaks and Tonbridge	1-85937-057-8	£12.99	Sep 99
					Sheffield and S Yorkshire	1-85937-070-5	£12.99	Sep 99
					Shropshire	1-85937-083-7	£14.99	Nov 99
					Southampton	1-85937-088-8	£12.99	Nov 99
					Staffordshire	1-85937-047-0	£14.99	Sep 99
					Stratford upon Avon	1-85937-098-5	£12.99	Nov 99
					Suffolk	1-85937-074-8	£14.99	Oct 99
					Surrey	1-85937-081-0	£14.99	Oct 99
					Torbay	1-85937-063-2	£12.99	Sep 99
					Wiltshire	1-85937-053-5	£14.99	Sep 99

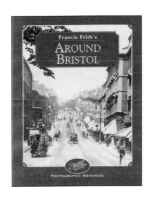
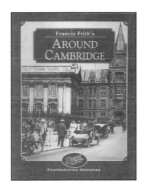

Derby	1-85937-046-2	£12.99	Sep 99
Devon	1-85937-052-7	£14.99	Sep 99
Dorset	1-85937-075-6	£14.99	Oct 99
Dorset Coast	1-85937-062-4	£14.99	Sep 99
Dublin	1-85937-058-6	£12.99	Sep 99
East Anglia	1-85937-059-4	£14.99	Sep 99
Eastbourne	1-85937-061-6	£12.99	Sep 99
English Castles	1-85937-078-0	£14.99	Oct 99
Essex	1-85937-082-9	£14.99	Nov 99
Falmouth	1-85937-066-7	£12.99	Sep 99
Hampshire	1-85937-064-0	£14.99	Sep 99
Hertfordshire	1-85937-079-9	£14.99	Nov 99
Isle of Man	1-85937-065-9	£14.99	Sep 99
Liverpool	1-85937-051-9	£12.99	Sep 99

British Life A Century Ago

246 x 189mm 144pp, hardback. Black and white Lavishly illustrated with photos from the turn of the century, and with extensive commentary. It offers a unique insight into the social history and heritage of bygone Britain.

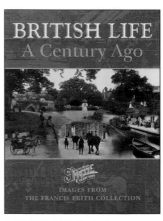

1-85937-103-5 £17.99 ....

Available from your local bookshop or from the publisher

FRITH PRODUCTS & SERVICES

Francis Frith would doubtless be pleased to know that the pioneering publishing venture he started in 1860 still continues today. More than a hundred and thirty years later, The Francis Frith Collection continues in the same innovative tradition and is now one of the foremost publishers of vintage photographs in the world. Some of the current activities include:

Interior Decoration

Today Frith's photographs can be seen framed and as giant wall murals in thousands of pubs, restaurants, hotels, banks, retail stores and other public buildings throughout the country. In every case they enhance the unique local atmosphere of the places they depict and provide reminders of gentler days in an increasingly busy and frenetic world.

Product Promotions

Frith products have been used by many major companies to promote the sales of their own products or to reinforce their own history and heritage. Brands include Hovis bread, Courage beers, Scotch Porage Oats, Colman's mustard, Cadbury's foods, Mellow Birds coffee, Dunhill pipe tobacco, Guinness, and Bulmer's Cider.

Genealogy and Family History

As the interest in family history and roots grows world-wide, more and more people are turning to Frith's photographs of Great Britain for images of the towns, villages and streets where their ancestors lived; and, of course, photographs of the churches and chapels where their ancestors were christened, married and buried are an essential part of every genealogy tree and family album.

A series of easy-to-use CD Roms is planned for publication, and an increasing number of Frith photographs will be able to be viewed on specialist genealogy sites. A growing range of Frith books will be available on CD.

The Internet

Already thousands of Frith photographs can be viewed and purchased on the internet. By the end of the year 2,000 some 60,000 Frith photographs will be available on the internet. The number of sites is constantly expanding, each focussing on different products and services from the Collection.

Some of the sites are listed below.

www.townpages.co.uk
www.familystorehouse.com
www.britannia.com
www.icollector.com
www.barclaysquare.co.uk
www.cornwall-online.co.uk

For background information on the Collection look at the two following sites:

www.francisfrith.com
www.francisfrith.co.uk

Frith Products

All Frith photographs are available Framed or just as Mounted Prints, and can be ordered from the address below. From time to time other products - Address Books, Calendars, Table Mats, Postcards etc - are available.

The Frith Collectors Guild

In response to the many customers who enjoy collecting Frith photographs we have created the Frith Collectors Guild. Members are entitled to a range of benefits, including a regular magazine, special discounts and special limited edition products.

For further information: if you would like further information on any of the above aspects of the Frith business please contact us at the address below:

The Francis Frith Collection, Frith's Barn, Teffont, Salisbury, Wiltshire England SP3 5QP.
Tel: +44 (0) 1722 716 376 Fax: +44 (0) 1722 716 881 Email: frithbook.co.uk

To receive your FREE Mounted Print

Cut out this Voucher and return it with your remittance for £1.50 to cover postage and handling. Choose any photograph included in this book. Your SEPIA print will be A4 in size, and mounted in a cream mount with burgundy rule lines, overall size 14 x 11 inches.

Order additional Mounted Prints at HALF PRICE (only £7.49 each*)

If there are further pictures you would like to order, possibly as gifts for friends and family, acquire them at half price (no additional postage and handling required).

Have your Mounted Prints framed*

For an additional £14.95 per print you can have your chosen Mounted Print framed in an elegant polished wood and gilt moulding, overall size 16 x 13 inches (no additional postage and handling required).

---

* IMPORTANT!
These special prices are only available if ordered using the original voucher on this page (no copies permitted) and at the same time as your free Mounted Print, for delivery to the same address

---

Voucher
for FREE and Reduced Price Frith Prints

Picture no.	Page number	Qty	Mounted @ £7.49	Framed + £14.95	Total Cost
		1	**Free of charge***	£	£
			£	£	£
			£	£	£
			£	£	£
			£	£	£
			£	£	£

Title: CHESHIRE
045-4

* Post & handling	£1.50
Total Order Cost	**£**

Please do not photocopy this voucher. Only the original is valid, so please cut it out and return it to us.

I enclose a cheque / postal order for £ . . . .
made payable to 'The Francis Frith Collection'
OR please debit my Mastercard / Visa / Switch / Amex card

Number . . . .

Expires . . . . Signature . . . .

Name Mr/Mrs/Ms . . . .

Address . . . .

. . . .

. . . .

. . . . Postcode . . . .

Daytime Tel No . . . .   Valid to 31/12/01

Frith Collectors' Guild

From time to time we publish a magazine of news and stories about Frith photographs and further special offers of Frith products. If you would like 12 months FREE membership, please return this form and we will send you a New Member Pack.

Send completed forms to:
**The Francis Frith Collection,
Frith's Barn, Teffont, Salisbury,
Wiltshire SP3 5QP**

The Francis Frith Collectors' Guild

I would like to receive the New Members Pack offering 12 months FREE membership.

045-4

Name Mr/Mrs/Ms . . . .

Address . . . .

. . . .

. . . .

. . . . Postcode . . . .

Free Print - see overleaf